D1510306

Celebrating Christmas

**Written and compiled
by Christina Goodings**

LION
Children's Books

Somerset County Library
Bridgewater, NJ   08807

To Lois, Nicky and Vic

Text copyright © 1998 Christina Goodings
Illustrations copyright © 1998 Helen Cann (pp. 2, 4–5, 84–88);
Elena Gomez (front cover, pp. 2, 44–45, 76–77); Susan Hutchison
(pp. 2, 20–25, 42–43, 49–51, 54, 58, 60, 62); Francesca Pelizzoli
(pp. 2, 10–13, 26–39, 96); Liz Pichon (pp. 2, 80–83); Claire St Louis
Little (pp. 2, 7, 89–95); Alison Wisenfeld (pp. 2, 78–79); Sarah Young
(pp. 2, 8, 46–48, 52, 56, 64, 66, 70, 73–75)
This edition copyright © 1999 Lion Publishing
Designed by Nicky Farthing
Photography by John Williams Studios, Thame

The moral rights of the author and illustrators
have been asserted

Published by
Lion Publishing
4050 Lee Vance View, Colorado Springs, CO 80918, USA
ISBN 0 7459 4090 0

First UK edition 1998
First US edition 1999
10 9 8 7 6 5 4 3 2 1 0

All rights reserved

Acknowledgments
Our grateful thanks to Sonning Common Primary School, England for
the Nativity scenes on pp. 14–29. Pupils who took part are as follows:
Amy Betts, Coral Bosley, Nicola Brakspear, Emily Brewer,
Claire Burnett, James Butler, Amy Charlesworth, Katy Clements,
Verity Cunningham, Michael Darnell, Georgia Dunk, Madeline Dykes,
Jack Griffiths, Samantha Jenkins, Jack Jiggens, Keli Jiggens, Katie Kenrick,
Jamie Knapp, Lawrence Parmenter, Jade Price, Toby Savin, Frances Shillito.
Special thanks to their teacher, Melanie Choules, and to Terri Jiggens.

Text Acknowledgments
'Nativity Play', copyright © 1996 Clare Bevan. Reproduced by
permission. 'Lucy's Carol' from *A Pocket Book of Spiritual Poems*
copyright © 1996 Rumer Godden. Reproduced by permission of
Hodder and Stoughton Limited, and Curtis Brown on behalf of
Rumer Godden. 'The Oxen' from *The Complete Poems by Thomas
Hardy* edited by James Gibson, Papermac 1978. Reproduced by
permission of Macmillan. 'Christmas' by Mary I. Osborne from
The Book of 1000 Poems—The Classic Collection for Children.
Reproduced by permission of HarperCollins Publishers Ltd.
'The Shepherds' Carol' from *The Witnesses and Other Poems* by
Clive Sansom, published by Methuen. Reprinted by permission
of David Higham Associates Limited.

Music Acknowledgments
Arrangement of 'Silent Night' copyright © 1998 Philip and Victoria
Tebbs, from *Best-Loved Carols*, published by Lion Publishing.

Library of Congress CIP data applied for

Printed and bound in Singapore

C o n t e n t s

Part One

Waiting for Christmas 5
'Winter Now' *Samuel Longfellow*
Illustrated by Helen Cann

★

Advent Lights 6
A Traditional Swedish Carol 7
Illustrated by Claire St Louis Little

Advent Stars 8
Illustrated by Sarah Young

The People Who Walked in Darkness *From the Bible* 10
Illustrated by Francesca Pelizzoli

Part Two

The Christmas Story 13
'An Azure Sky' *Mary I. Osborne*
Illustrated by Francesca Pelizzoli

★

'Nativity Play' *Clare Bevan* 14
Photographed at Sonning Common Primary School

Tunics 20
Costume Extras 22

The Birth of Jesus Christ *From the Bible* 26
Section illustrated by Francesca Pelizzoli

'I Sing of a Maiden' *Anonymous* 27

The Baby in the Manger *From the Bible* 28

'Love Came Down at Christmas' *Christina Rossetti* 29

The Shepherds on the Hillside *From the Bible* 30

'The Shepherds' Carol' *Clive Sansom* 31

A Story of Mary and Joseph *From the Bible* 32

Illustrated by

Elena Gomez

Susan Hutchison

Francesca Pelizzoli

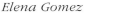

'Lucy's Carol' *Lucy, aged five* 33

The Wise Men and King Herod *From the Bible* 34

'Carol of the Wise Men' *Traditional English* 35

The Wise Men and Their Gifts *From the Bible* 36

'A Child's Gift' *Christina Rossetti* 37

'Silent Night' *Joseph Mohr* 38

A Nativity Scene 40

Outlines for the Nativity Scene 42

Part Three

Christmas Festivity 45

'The Golden Gift Box' *Lois Rock*
Illustrated by Elena Gomez

★

The Christmas Tree 46
Section illustrated by
Susan Hutchison & Sarah Young

Tree Decorations 48

Christmas Cards 52

Envelopes 54

Make Your Own Gift-wrap 56

Wrapping Gifts 58

Gift Bags 60

Christmas Stockings 62

Christmas Gifts 64

Christmas Goodies 68

Christmas Drinks 72

Part Four

Tales and Legends 75

'Our Saviour's Birth…' *William Shakespeare*
Illustrated by Sarah Young

★

'The Oxen' *Thomas Hardy* 76
Illustrated by Elena Gomez

'All in Tune' *Anonymous* 78
Illustrated by Alison Wisenfeld

The Baker's Christmas *Christina Goodings* 80
Illustrated by Liz Pichon

The Legend of Saint Nicholas *Lois Rock* 84
Illustrated by Helen Cann

The Tale of Three Trees *Mary Joslin* 89
Illustrated by Claire St Louis Little

'A Christmas Prayer' *Robert Louis Stephenson* 96
Illustrated by Francesca Pelizzoli

 This symbol indicates a craft page

Sarah Young

Alison Wisenfeld

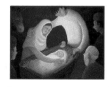

Claire St Louis Little

Helen Cann

Liz Pichon

PART 1

Waiting for Christmas

'Tis winter now; the fallen snow
* Has left the heavens all coldly clear;*
Through leafless boughs the sharp winds blow,
* And all the earth lies dead and drear.*

And yet God's love is not withdrawn;
* His life within the keen air breathes;*
His beauty paints the crimson dawn,
* And clothes the boughs with glittering wreaths.*

And though abroad the sharp winds blow,
* And skies are chill, and frosts are keen,*
Home closer draws her circle now,
* And warmer glows her light within.*

O God! who giv'st the winter's cold,
* As well as summer's joyous rays,*
Us warmly in thy love enfold,
* And keep us through life's wintry days.*

SAMUEL LONGFELLOW (1819–92)

Advent Lights

Will it ever be Christmas?

As winter casts its shadow over the world, the waiting time seems so long: the days are cold and bleak; the nights are long and dark.

The four weeks before Christmas are the season of Advent. 'Advent' means 'coming' and it is a time to get ready for the celebrations ahead. Advent traditions help mark each passing day.

You will need:

★ *24 candles (or as many as you need to count the days till Christmas)*

★ *small terracotta flowerpots— one for each candle*

★ *damp sand or soil*

★ *a terracotta plant tray to hold all your pots safely*

★ *evergreen foliage*

1. Half-fill the tray with sand and wedge all the pots upright in it. Fill the pots about two-thirds full of sand.

2. Poke a little evergreen foliage into the sand in the tray. Make sure it is low enough not to catch alight as the candles burn.

3. Put one candle in each pot.

4. Light one candle on December 1. Enjoy watching it burn for a few minutes, then blow it out. On December 2, light two candles— and continue lighting one more candle each day to help you look forward to the Christmas celebrations.

★ Remember to keep the sand moist by adding a little water each day to make the foliage last longer.

A Traditional Swedish Carol

★

Now light one thousand Christmas lights
On dark earth here tonight;
One thousand, thousand also shine
To make the dark sky bright.

Oh, once when skies were starry bright,
In stable cold and bare,
Sweet Mary bore a son that night,
A child both kind and fair.

He came to bring us love and light
To bring us peace on earth,
So let your candles shine tonight
And sing with joy and mirth.

Advent Stars

You will need:

★ *4 letter or legal-sized pieces of thick watercolour paper or thin card*

★ *scissors*

★ *plate, about 8 inches in diameter*

★ *pencil*

★ *tracing-paper*

★ *pin with a large coloured head*

★ *flat piece of polystyrene or pad made from several layers of thick, soft paper*

★ *hanging thread*

★ *clear sticky-tape*

1. Lay the plate on one of the pieces of paper and draw a circle. Cut it out.

2. Mark a spiral inwards. Cut along the line. Tape a length of hanging thread to the centre of the spiral. Hang the bare spiral in a place you can reach.

3. Trace the star shape shown here and copy it onto a piece of thick paper or card. Cut this star out as carefully as possible, as you need to use it as a template.

4. Using the template to draw round, draw as many stars are there are days to Christmas. Cut them out.

5. Lay one star on the polystyrene and prick out a pattern. The examples shown here give some ideas for you to copy, but you can easily make up designs of your own.

6. Make pinprick designs on all the stars. You can do this all at once—but you may decide to do just one design each day .

7. Cut a piece of hanging thread 8 inches long. Tape one end to a star and the other to the spiral.

★ Hang one star every day. Start at the bottom, and hang stars further and further up the spiral as Christmas comes nearer and nearer.

The People Who Walked in Darkness

★

Adapted from the Bible
Illustrated by Francesca Pelizzoli

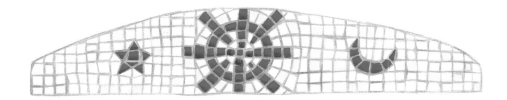

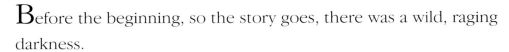

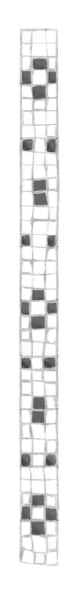

Before the beginning, so the story goes, there was a wild, raging darkness.

The great Maker God spoke. God commanded light to appear, and the light came.

God spoke again, creating earth and sky, and God made the sun, moon and stars that dance in dazzling circles through the vast universe.

God made the whole world, both land and sea, and filled them with every kind of living thing. Soon, slender green shoots unfurled their leaves; flowers blossomed in a festival of colour; fruits ripened in the golden sun. Strange and beautiful animals with softly flickering eyes trod the soft earth. Birds filled the air with their songs, their haunting, hooting, shrilling, trilling, warbling cries; and in the cool green waters shimmered the great shoals of fish.

Then, God made people to take care of the world. It was to be their safe and lovely home. They were to live as friends of God and know joy and happiness.

But the people grew proud. They thought they had no need of their Maker. They began to live selfishly, greedily plundering the world and fighting with one another.

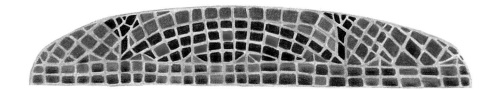

Then the shadow of sadness came upon the earth: weeping and sorrow; darkness and death.

In the fullness of time, God made a promise. It was told and retold by prophets, who heard God speaking to them. 'This what God says,' they proclaimed, 'a child will be born on earth—God's chosen one. He will lead people out of the darkness of their sorrow and into the light of happiness. When that happens, there will once again be joy and peace…'

★

'The people who walked in darkness have seen a great light;
those who lived in a land of deep darkness—
on them light has shined…
For a child has been born for us,
a son given to us;
authority rests upon his shoulders;
and he is named Wonderful Counsellor,
Mighty God, Everlasting Father, Prince of Peace.'

ISAIAH 9:2, 6

PART 2

The Christmas Story

An azure sky,
All star bestrewn.
A lowly crib,
A hushed room.
An open door,
A hill afar,
Where little lambs
And shepherds are.
To such a world,
On such a night,
Came Jesus—
Little Lord of Light.

MARY I. OSBORNE

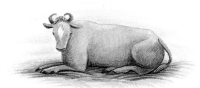

Nativity Play

★

Clare Bevan

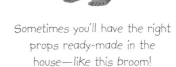

*H*ere is an inn with a stable,
Equipped with some straw and a chair.
Here is an angel in bed sheets,
With tinsel to tie back her hair.

Here is a servant in bath towels
Who sweeps round the stage with a broom.
Here is a chorus of faces
All eager to cry out, 'NO ROOM!'

Here is a Joseph who stammers,
And tries to remember his lines.
Here is a teacher in anguish,
Who frantically gestures and signs.

An angel costume made from
two rectangles of white fabric
simply knotted at the shoulder
and held in place with a sash.

Sometimes you'll have the right
props ready-made in the
house—like this broom!

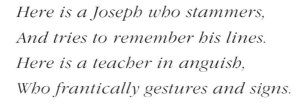

A tunic with sleeves and a tie belt plus
a sleeveless coat looks special, but is
still very easy to make (see p. 2!).

(see p. 2!)

Note to all grown-ups in charge
of a Nativity play:
The lines the children invent are
always enjoyed the most!

Here is 'Away In A Manger'—
A tune MOST recorders can play.
Here is the moment of wonder,
As Jesus appears in the hay.

Here is a Mary with freckles
Whose baby is plastic and hard.
Here is a donkey in trousers,
With ears made from pieces of card.

Away in a manger, no crib for a bed,
The little Lord Jesus laid down his sweet head;
The stars in the bright sky looked down where he lay,
The little Lord Jesus asleep on the hay.

Baggy clothes in the right colour
and cardboard ears make a
simple but recognizable costume.

Mary's tunic is traditionally in
blue. Her head-dress is a square
of cloth folded diagonally to make
a triangle and simply draped.

This manger is made from two
painted cardboard fruit trays, with
one placed on top of the other.

A crook can be made from coathanger wire bent into shape and tied to a thick dowel with string. The addition of a woolly sock makes it less dangerous.

Here is a shepherd in curtains,
Who carries a crook made of wire.
Here is a boy sucking cough sweets,
Who growls from the back of the choir.

Here is a King bearing bath salts,
Who points at a star hung on strings.
Here is a dove who has stage fright,
And quivers her crêpe-paper wings.

Oversized socks pulled up over the arms make a sheep costume more fun!

Loops of wool hold the dove's wings to her wrists, so she can 'flap' daintily.

Long-sleeved tunics in rich-looking fabrics are ideal for the 'wise men', and left-over fabric can be used for turban hats.

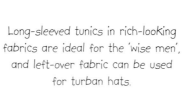

A plain T-shirt and a towel tunic is the quickest way to the 'Nativity Play' look!

Simple animal costumes work especially well if the wearer acts the part. Here is a humpy, grumpy camel!

Here is a page boy in plimsolls
Who stumbles his way up the stairs.
Here is a long line of cherubs
Who march round the manger in pairs.

Here is a camel who fidgets,
With plasters stuck over his knee.
Here are some sheep who just giggle,
And think no one out there can see.

Here is a Herod in glasses
Who whispers, so nobody hears.
Here is a Mum with a hanky,
To cover her pride and her tears.

It's an enjoyable luxury to have a Nativity play costume properly sewn from specially purchased fabric. .

Is she laughing?
Is she crying?

Cherubs in T-shirts and tights...

...with gold wings neatly tied on.

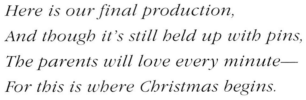

Here is our final production,
And though it's still held up with pins,
The parents will love every minute—
For this is where Christmas begins.

They can sing and dance through the play...

...but sometimes their wings might
need adjusting!

EVERYBODY wants to be in the group shot. There's always someone who isn't looking quite the way the photographer planned—but everyone looks great. Well done to all those on stage and behind the scenes who worked to make this year's play so special!

★ *Towel tunics*

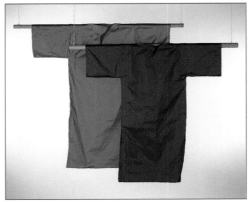

★ *Long-sleeved tunics*

★ *Long-sleeved tunic and coat*

Tunics

Tunics are the basis for nearly all the costumes for the Nativity play. The very simplest are made from two rectangles of fabric (such as towels) pinned at the shoulder and held in place with a belt.

You will need:

★ *fabric (allow between 1 and 2 metres for any of the designs shown here, depending on the size of the child, the length you require, and whether or not you are making one with sleeves)*

★ *measuring-tape*

★ *long ruler*

★ *marking-chalk*

★ *thread*

★ *scissors*

★ *needle/sewing-machine*

A Stitched Tunic

1. The stitched tunic is also made from two rectangles of fabric. Each needs to be wide enough to reach from the middle of one upper arm to the other, and from shoulder height to as long as you want it. Mark the size of the rectangle in chalk on your fabric with a ruler, taking care to ensure that the edges line up with the weave of the fabric.

2. Cut the shapes out.

3. Put right sides together and stitch together at the shoulders for a few centimetres. You need to leave a large opening for the neck, but not so large the tunic slips off the shoulders.

4. Still with right sides together, stitch the sides, leaving a large opening for the arms. If you wish, leave the tunic open at the sides from knee to hem so it is easy to walk in.

5. Turn right side out. If you wish, turn down the raw edges at the neck and sleeve openings and stitch them down. Fold a hem and stitch that in place if you wish.

Never make a tunic too long. If the wearer has to go up any steps, it is a good idea to cut it no longer than mid-calf at the front.

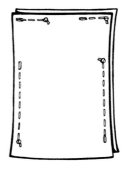

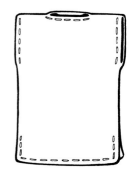

If you stitch the raw edges in place, you might like to choose a contrasting thread.

Long-sleeved Tunic

Make the armhole quite deep— if too small, it can be a nuisance!

Taper the sleeve by 2–5 mm either side.

1. Cut two rectangles of fabric as for the simplest tunic.

2. Then cut two pieces for the sleeves. Measure from just above the waist over the shoulder and down to the same point above the waist. Then measure from the wearer's elbow to the wearer's wrist. Cut two rectangles to these measurements.

3. Lay the sleeve pieces flat and taper evenly as shown.

4. Join the shoulder seams as described for the simplest tunic. Then lay the joined piece right side up and centre the sleeve pieces on it, right sides together. Sew the seam.

5. Next, fold the tunic and stitch the sleeve and side seams.

6. If you wish, turn in the edges and stitch.

Coat

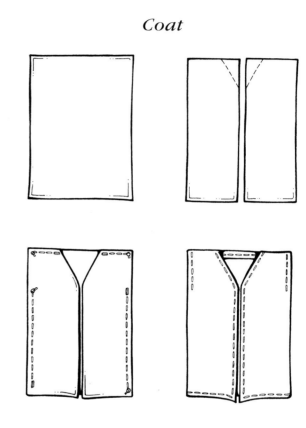

Making a 'V' neck is useful if the wrong side of the fabric is unattractive and you don't want it to show. Otherwise you can leave the front edges straight.

1. This coat is made from two rectangles like the simplest tunic. Measure as for the tunic in order to get the right size of rectangle.

2. Cut one piece down the middle to give two front pieces.

3. If you wish, trim the neck as shown into a 'V'.

4. For a neat finish, turn in the cut edges and stitch in place.

★ *Head-dress*

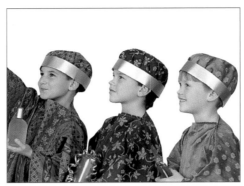

★ *Turban hats*

★ *Crown*

Costume Extras

The right headgear adds a great deal to the effectiveness of a costume. Here are some ideas—but you can invent your own with the materials you have to hand.

Head-dress

1. Fold a square of cloth into a triangle to make a working man's head-dress.

2. Make a knotted band using strips cut from old tights or slightly stretchy braided shoelaces.

3. Knot the band into a circle to fit the wearer and use it to hold the cloth in place.

Turban Hats

1. Cut a strip of plain card about 3 cm high and long enough to fit round the wearer's head with enough overlap so you can join it.

2. Tape or staple it into a circle.

3. Drape the cloth or paper over the wearer's head and push the card circle over it. Use chalk to mark a line just below the card.

4. Remove the circle and the cloth. Use the chalk mark as a guide to cutting a near-circular shape. Note the centre front and centre back points.

5. Staple the cloth evenly into the inside of the card circle, marking the centre front and centre back.

Ensure the smooth side of the staples is to the wearer's head.

6. Cut a strip of metallic card as long as the plain card and 7 cm deep. Fold it in half lengthways. Notch one long edge, as shown below.

7. Slot the folded card over the plain card, with the notches inside. Hold in place with a staple at the centre back, centre front and either side.

8. Cover the staples with masking tape on the inside and stickers on the outside, if you wish.

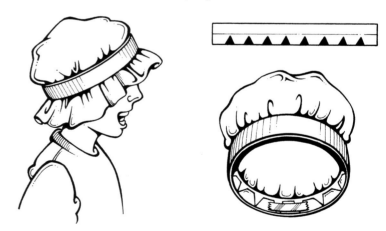

Crown

1. Cut a rectangle of metallic card long enough to fit round the wearer's head with a slight overlap.

2. Lay the card flat and mark deep 'V's along the top edge. Cut out.

3. Tape the crown into a circle.

★ *Sheep hats with silly ears*   ★ *Camel hat with card ears*   ★ *Donkey hat with long card ears*

Plain Hats

Plain hats in the right coloured fabric are useful for animal costumes. Sheep, camels and donkeys are just a few ideas.

1. Cut a rectangle 300 x 450 cm.

2. Fold in half lengthways and stitch up the sides.

3. Stitch a 3 cm triangle off each top corner and trim the spare fabric away. Turn right side out.

4. Try the hat on the wearer. It is easy to make any adjustments to the top by re-stitching: simply trim extra fabric away when the fit is right. If you wish, you can hem the bottom edge.

3. For the best fit, put the headband on the wearer and mark where *their* ears are. Tape the card ears at these points.

Sheep Hats

1. Make the plain hat to stage 2 and then turn right side out. Tie off the triangle shape at each top corner to make ears.

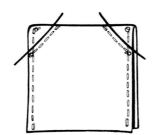

Card Ears

1. Cut a strip of card 3 cm deep and long enough to fit around the wearer's head with a slight overlap. Tape in place.

2. Draw the ear shape you require on plain paper until you think it looks right. Then use this as a pattern to cut two ears in card.

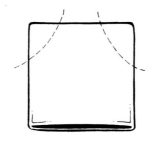

Polyester batting or fleece make great sheep hats!

★ *When you need a lot of costumes...*   *find the simplest solution...*   *with just one special thing to make.*

Cherub Wings

1. Make cherub wings from double-sided gold card. As the wings need to be quite stiff, it is quite a good idea to make your own doubled-sided card by glueing two single-sided sheets together.

2. Draw a shape similar to the one shown below and cut it out.

3. Now make a ribbon tie. Fold 6 m gold ribbon in half and tie an overhand knot to leave a loop about 2 cm long in the middle.

4. Centre the knotted ribbon on the wrong side of the wing piece so the loop extends below the card, and fasten with packing tape. Make another overhand knot at the top.

5. Wrap the ribbon around the wearer, as shown, to attach the wings.

★ *Cherubs*

★ *Dove*

★ *Angel*

Dove Wings

Crêpe paper dove wings are made rather like the cherub wings.

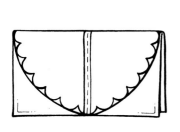

★ *Dove wings and cherub wings*

1. Overlap two folded pieces of white crêpe paper—together they need to reach from one outstretched wrist of the wearer to the other. Join them with two rows of a large in-and-out tucking stitch. Cut the piece into a large semicircle.

2. Pull the tacking thread to gather the crêpe paper. Fix the gathered part onto a strip of card 3 cm x 15 cm using a long machine stitch or staples.

3. Add a white wool tie, made in the same way as the gold ribbon tie that attaches the cherub wings.

4. Add loops of wool at the wing-tips to hold the wings to the arms.

Angel Wings

A metre of gauzy fabric can be worn as 'wings'.

1. Knot the corners as shown.

2. The wearer puts their arms through the holes, waistcoat-fashion.

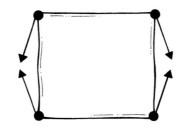

The Birth of Jesus Christ

✦

*Adapted from the Gospel according
to St Luke, in the Bible*

*The story takes place in the land that lies at the eastern shore of the
Mediterranean Sea. It was known as Palestine; its people were the people
of Israel, who were also known as the Jews. The northern region was
called Galilee and the southern region was called Judea. It all belonged
to the mighty Roman Empire.*

The angel Gabriel was sent by God to a young woman named Mary
in the town of Nazareth, in Galilee. She was engaged to Joseph, a
descendant of the great King David, who had lived and reigned a
thousand years earlier.

'Peace be with you!' the angel said to her. 'The Lord is with you, and
has greatly blessed you.'

The words were good and gentle, but Mary was deeply troubled.
What did this mean? What was going to happen to her?

'Do not be afraid,' said the angel. 'God has chosen you to bear a
son, and you will call him Jesus. He will be great; he will be called
the Son of the Most High, and he will be a king, as was his ancestor
David. But he will rule for ever; his kingdom will never end.'

Mary was puzzled. 'How can this be?' she asked the angel. 'I'm not
yet a wife; I'm still a virgin, so how can I become a mother?'

The angel answered, 'The Holy Spirit will come on you and God's
power will rest upon you. For this reason, the holy child will be
called the Son of God.'

Mary replied, 'Behold, here I am, the handmaid of the Lord—God's
servant. Let everything happen as you have said.'

And the angel departed.

LUKE 1:26–38

I Sing of a Maiden

★

Anonymous (15th century)

I sing of a maiden
  That is matchless:
King of all kings
  For her son she ches. *

He came all so stillè
  Where his mother was,
As dew in Aprillè
  That falls on the grass.

He came all so stillè
  To his mother's bower,
As dew in Aprillè
  That falls on the flower.

He came all so stillè
  Where his mother lay,
As dew in Aprillè
  That falls on the spray.

Mother and maiden
  Was never none but she
Well may such a lady
  God's mother be.

* ches: choose

The Baby in the Manger

✶

*Adapted from the Gospel according
to St Luke, in the Bible*

In those days, a decree went out from the Emperor Augustus that everybody in the Roman Empire should be registered, each in their own town. So Joseph left Nazareth in Galilee to go to Judea, to the city of David called Bethlehem, because he was descended from the family of David. He went with Mary, to whom he was engaged. She was expecting a baby.

While they were there, the time came for her to deliver her child. She gave birth to a son, her first-born. She wrapped him in bands of cloth, and laid in a manger, because there was no place for them in the inn.

LUKE 2:1–7

Love Came Down at Christmas

★

Christina Rossetti (1830–94)

Love came down at Christmas,
   Love all lovely, Love Divine;
Love was born at Christmas,
   Star and Angels gave the sign.

Worship we the Godhead,
   Love Incarnate, Love Divine;
Worship we our Jesus:
   But wherewith for sacred sign?

Love shall be our token,
   Love be yours and love be mine,
Love to God and all men,
   Love for plea and gift and sign.

The Shepherds on the Hillside

★

Adapted from the Gospel according
to St Luke, in the Bible

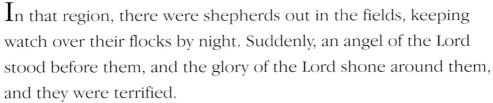

In that region, there were shepherds out in the fields, keeping watch over their flocks by night. Suddenly, an angel of the Lord stood before them, and the glory of the Lord shone around them, and they were terrified.

But the angel said to them, 'Do not be afraid—I am bringing you good news of great joy for all people: today, in the city of David, a Saviour has been born for you, who is the Christ, the Lord. This will be the sign: you will find a baby wrapped in bands of cloth and lying in a manger.'

Suddenly there was with the angel a great multitude of the heavenly host praising God and saying, 'Glory to God in the highest heaven, and on earth peace among those with whom God is pleased.'

When the angels had left them and gone to heaven, the shepherds said to one another, 'Let us go now to Bethlehem and see this thing that has taken place, which the Lord has told us about.'

So they hurried to Bethlehem and found Mary and Joseph, and the baby lying in the manger. They explained all they had been told about the child, and everyone who heard their story was amazed.

Mary treasured their words, and pondered them deeply in her heart.

Then the shepherds returned to their sheep, praising God for all they had seen and heard.

LUKE 2:8–20

The Shepherds' Carol

★

Clive Sansom

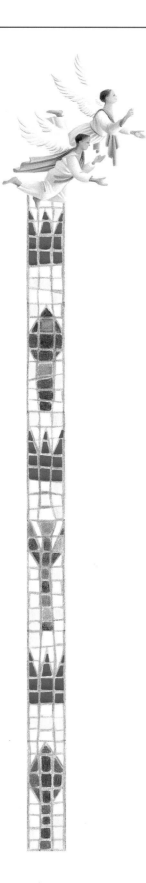

We stood on the hills, Lady,
  Our day's work done,
Watching the frosted meadows
  That winter had won.

The evening was calm, Lady,
  The air so still,
Silence more lovely than music
  Folded the hill.

There was a star, Lady,
  Shone in the night.
Larger than Venus it was
  And bright, so bright—

Oh, a voice from the sky, Lady,
  It seemed to us then,
Telling of God being born
  In the world of men.

And so, we have come, Lady,
  Our day's work done:
Our love, our hopes, our selves
  We give to your son.

A Story of Mary and Joseph

✶

*Adapted from the Gospel according
to St Matthew, in the Bible*

Here is another account of the same story attributed to Matthew.

This was how the birth of Jesus Christ took place. His mother Mary was engaged to Joseph, but before they were married, Mary found she was pregnant, by means of the Holy Spirit.

Joseph was a good man. He did not want Mary to be publicly disgraced, so he planned to break off the engagement quietly.

He had just made up his mind to do this when an angel of the Lord appeared to him in a dream. The angel said, 'Joseph, son of David, do not be afraid to take Mary as your wife. The child she carries is from the Holy Spirit. She will bear a son, and you are to name him Jesus, for he will save his people from their sins.'

When Joseph awoke, he did what the angel had told him to do.

MATTHEW 1:18–25

Lucy's Carol

★

Lucy was five years old when she composed this carol;
her mother wrote it down word for word.

W*hen the Baby borned*
Joseph said to Mary,
'What am I going to do about
This little-born Jesus Baby Christ?
I never knew it was going to be like this,
With all these angels and kings
And shepherds and stars and things;
It's got me worried, I can tell you,
On Christmas Day in the morning.'

Mary said to Joseph,
'Not to worry, my darling,
Dear old darling Joseph;
Everything's going to be all right,
Because the Angel told me not to fear;
So just hold up the lamp,
So I can see the dear funny sweet little face
Of my darling little-born Jesus Baby Christ.'

Joseph said to Mary,
'Behold the handyman of the Lord!'

Happy Christmas, happy Christmas!
Christ is born today.

The Wise Men and King Herod

★

*Adapted from the Gospel according
to St Matthew, in the Bible*

Jesus was born in Bethlehem, in Judaea, at the time when Herod was king. Herod had won his power by scheming, currying favour with the Romans who controlled the Empire. His palace towers stood out proudly on the skyline of the capital city of Jerusalem; yet Herod lived in fear that others would overthrow him.

To the city of Jerusalem came wise men came from the East. They were astrologers who studied the night sky and looked for meanings in the patterns of the stars, and they were on a quest. 'Where is the child who has been born king of the Jews?' they asked. 'We have seen his star in the East and have come to pay him homage.'

When King Herod heard this, he was frightened. (So were all the people of Jerusalem, for when King Herod was angry, no one was safe.) He called together his chief priests and scholars. 'I recall that our prophets foretell the birth of a king,' he said, 'God's chosen king. Where do they say he will be born?'

'In Bethlehem of Judea,' they replied, and they read aloud words from the book of one of their ancient prophets:
' "And you, Bethlehem, in the land of Judah,
are by no means least among the rulers of Judah;
For from you shall come a ruler
who is to shepherd my people Israel." '

Then Herod secretly called for the wise men and learned from them the exact time when the star had appeared. He sent them to Bethlehem, which was just a short journey away, saying, 'Go and search for the child; and when you have found him bring me word so that I may also go and pay him homage.'

MATTHEW 2:1–8

Carol of the Wise Men

★

Traditional English

*T*he star we've waited for so long
To tell us of his coming,
Is here! Is here! And we must go
With trumpets and drums drumming!
The star we follow on this night
Will lead us to the cradle,
Where he was born this holy night
In poor and lowly stable.

The way is long, the way is cold,
We cannot tarry longer,
The birth of him the star has told
The way is still much longer.
A king is born this holy morn
And gifts to him we're bringing.
The child we've waited for is born!
Oh hear the angels singing!

The Wise Men and Their Gifts

★

*Adapted from the Gospel according
to St Matthew, in the Bible*

The wise men set out. There, ahead of them, was the star they had seen before. They were filled with great joy. Soon, the star stopped over a house. They went in and saw the baby with his mother Mary. They knelt down and paid him homage. Then they opened their treasure chests and offered him gifts of gold, frankincense and myrrh.

When the wise men had given these gifts to Jesus, they did not return to Herod. A dream had warned them not to do so, and they left for their own country by another road.

After they had left, an angel of the Lord appeared to Joseph in a dream. The angel said, 'Get up, take the child and his mother, and flee to Egypt, and remain there until I tell you, for Herod plans to find the child and kill him.' Joseph did as the angel said, and stayed in Egypt until he heard that Herod had died.

MATTHEW 2:9–15

A Child's Gift

★

Christina Rossetti (1830–94)

What can I give him,
Poor as I am?
If I were a shepherd
I would bring a lamb;
If I were a wise man
I would do my part;
Yet what I can I give him—
Give my heart.

Silent Night

★

Joseph Mohr (1792–1848)
Translation: Anonymous

Silent night, holy night,
All is calm, all is bright
Round yon virgin mother and child;
Holy infant so tender and mild,
Sleep in heavenly peace,
Sleep in heavenly peace.

Silent night, holy night,
Shepherds quake at the sight;
Glories stream from heaven afar,
Heavenly hosts sing alleluia;
Christ, the Saviour, is born.
Christ, the Saviour, is born.

Silent night, holy night,
Son of God, love's pure light
Radiant beams from thy holy face,
With the dawn of redeeming grace,
Jesus, Lord, at thy birth,
Jesus, Lord, at thy birth.

Tune: Franz Grüber (1787–1863)
Arranged by Philip and Victoria Tebbs, copyright © 1998

A Nativity Scene

A Nativity scene is a traditional decoration which retells the Christmas story of the birth of Jesus. It is possible to buy very beautiful and elaborately made figures; but one that is hand-made by people who are having fun celebrating Christmas together is a priceless treasure.

A Nativity scene traditionally includes the following:

* stable in Bethlehem

* Mary and Joseph

* baby Jesus, wrapped in swaddling clothes and lying in a manger

* animals in the stable

* visiting shepherds and their sheep

* angels

* three wise men, bearing gifts for the baby.

The outlines on the next page will help you create your own version.

Outlines for the Nativity Scene

These outlines show clearly how to make a stable and figures that really stand up. You can copy the figures exactly if you like, using tracing paper, or design your own variations. Keep the overall size of each figure roughly the same as the guide, or you may end up creating something that is top-heavy and topples.

The tab at the foot of each figure needs to be slit in the middle. One part is decorated to look like part of the floor and is bent forward. The other part is bent back, to balance the figure. Any figure that keeps falling over can be held more firmly with a little sticky putty underneath each tab.

Fold back

Glue here

Fold back

Arrange the figures to make the scene come alive.

Cut slit in sky. Tuck angel in place.

Fold back

Fold back

Fold back

Fold back

Glue here

When you have made your figures, copy or trace the stable outline and colour it in. Fold along the lines. Then fold the tabs and glue them to the underside of the floor. If you use sticky putty, you can remove it after Christmas and use the stable again another year.

PART 3
Christmas Festivity

It's Christmas time,
When angels come
To earth from heaven above.
Take a golden gift box
And fill it full of love.

It's Christmas time!
The angels' song
Is heard upon the ground.
Open up the gift box,
Let love shine all around.

LOIS ROCK

The Christmas Tree

You can make a tiny tree by this method, or one over 2 metres tall! You need to decide how tall you want your poles to be, and then find a pot big enough to hold them.

You will need:

★ *6–8 bamboo poles*

★ *gesso*

★ *acrylic paint*

★ *paintbrushes*

★ *cord, twine or raffia*

★ *scissors*

★ *flowerpot*

★ *soil*

Everyone can make a tree that is sized just right for them with this simple design.

 Mix and match the colours of your string, poles and pots whichever way you wish.

1. Paint the poles with gesso and leave to dry. Then apply a coat of paint and leave that to dry. Apply a second coat.

2. Paint the pot to match if you wish.

3. Fill the flowerpot with soil and insert the poles as shown. Pack the soil around them quite firmly. Tie them together at the top with a piece of cord unwound from the ball.

4. Now unwind the ball as you spiral the cord down around the poles as shown. Take a few extra turns at the base of the poles. Then spiral the cord upwards to the top.

5. At the top, wind the cord around the poles for a few turns to hold them tight. Knot the ends together and tuck any dangling pieces inside the tree.

The following pages explain how to make decorations like these. You can easily tie or peg them to this tree design.

Tree Decorations

You will need:

* ★ *double-sided craft foil or paper (see this page)*
* ★ *white cartridge paper*
* ★ *plain white paper*
* ★ *craft knife and cutting-board or scissors*
* ★ *ruler*
* ★ *pencil*
* ★ *sticky-tape*
* ★ *thread for hanging your decorations*
* ★ *water-based paint*
* ★ *large, soft paintbrush*
* ★ *sponge*
* ★ *pair of compasses*

Double-sided Paper

1. Brush one side of some white cartridge paper with paint. Dip the bristles of your paintbrush in the paint, and then brush out the colour to give a streaky effect, with the brush strokes all running diagonally across the paper. Leave the paint to dry completely.

2. Barely dip the brush in more paint and brush diagonally across in the other direction. Leave to dry.

3. Turn the paper over and sponge the other side. Lightly dip a sponge in the paint and dab it on the paper to give a mottled effect.

Stars

1. First you need to make triangles from your chosen paper or foil. Use a pair of compasses to draw a circle on plain white paper. Choose a radius of 6 or 8 cm.

2. Keep the radius the same as you place the point on the edge of the circle and draw an arc with the pencil. Move the point to the arc and draw another. Repeat around the edge.

3. Now draw the lines as shown to make a triangle. Cut out and use as a template.

4. Fold each triangle (see below).

5. Gently unfold one side. Cut a length of thread, fold it in half and tape it in place as a loop that emerges from a folded point. Refold the side.

6. Tuck the inner edges so they nestle over and under each other as shown.

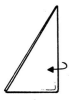

Fold the right corner to the left and make a short crease to mark the centre of the base.

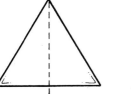

Fold the top point down to the crease mark.

Fold the right and left hand triangles over and crease. Unfold them.

Unfold the top triangle so the top third of the triangle sticks out to make a point.

Repeat for the other two corners.

Bags

1. Cut squares from your chosen paper or foil. The bags here were made from 15 cm squares.

2.

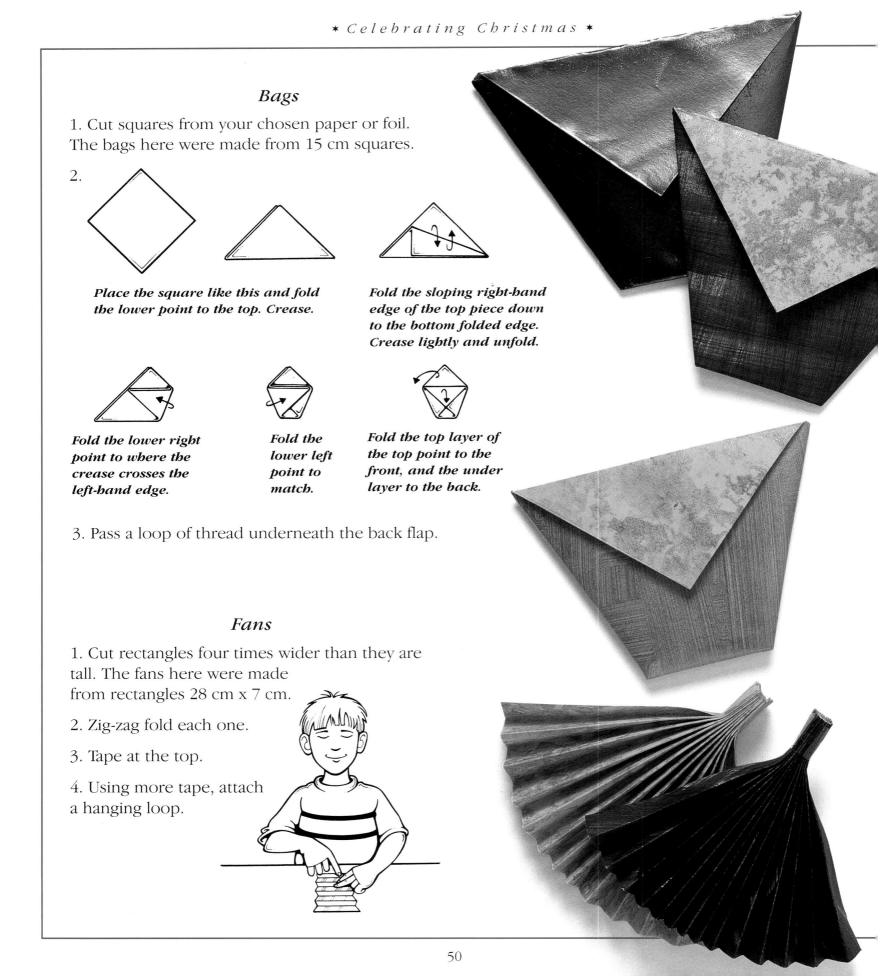

Place the square like this and fold the lower point to the top. Crease.

Fold the sloping right-hand edge of the top piece down to the bottom folded edge. Crease lightly and unfold.

Fold the lower right point to where the crease crosses the left-hand edge.

Fold the lower left point to match.

Fold the top layer of the top point to the front, and the under layer to the back.

3. Pass a loop of thread underneath the back flap.

Fans

1. Cut rectangles four times wider than they are tall. The fans here were made from rectangles 28 cm x 7 cm.

2. Zig-zag fold each one.

3. Tape at the top.

4. Using more tape, attach a hanging loop.

Paper Stockings

1. Cut squares. The stockings here were made from 18 cm squares.

2. Fold.

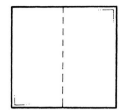

Fold in half length-ways and unfold.

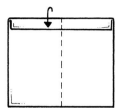

Fold down 1 cm for the border. Turn the paper over.

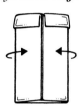

Fold the sides to the centre. Crease.

Fold the bottom corners in.

Fold the bottom point up to the point shown.

Fold the lower edge up to the top edge and crease.

Fold the flap back down so the shaped part juts below the rest.

Fold the right half over the left.

pull

Hold the 'leg' shut. Swivel out the 'foot'.

...tuck

Tuck the top layer of the stocking into the cuff of the under layer.

3. Attach a hanging loop with tape.

Christmas Cards

Make simple cards to send Christmas greetings to friends and relatives, near and far.

You will need:

★ *thick water-colour paper or thin card*

★ *oddments of paper with interesting textures*

★ *craft knife and cutting-board or scissors*

★ *pencil*

★ *ruler*

★ *glue*

Simple designs can be very effective

1. On your thick paper or thin card, mark a rectangle that will fold to the size of card you want. Cut it out on the board, carefully using a craft knife against the edge of the ruler (or cut out with scissors).

2. Mark the centre of the top and bottom edges. Score lightly with the knife or a pencil, using the ruler as a guide. Fold along the groove.

3. Tear squares or rectangles to make the coloured background for the card. Use the ruler as shown to guide the line of the tear. You can lightly mark the shape you want to tear with a pencil if you wish.

4. Tear simple shapes from smaller oddments of paper. Using your thumbs and forefingers, tear just a couple of millimetres each time to make the shape you want.

4. Assemble your card, using some of the ideas shown here. Experiment with your own designs.

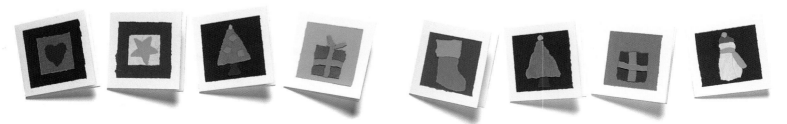

Envelopes

Make envelopes that are just the right size for your hand-made cards.

You will need:

★ *sheet of paper at least twice the size of your folded card*

★ *large piece of scrap paper*

★ *scissors*

★ *scraps of paper*

★ *glue stick*

You will need to experiment with a piece of scrap paper to work out just the right size for your envelope. Follow the instructions through with a scrap piece and trim the paper to the right size. When you have got it right, use the real paper. Use the scrap paper as a cutting guide for as many envelopes as you need in that size.

1. Centre the card on the envelope paper. (If you want to line the envelope, cut a piece of lining paper about 1 cm smaller all round than the envelope paper and glue it in place. Continue with the instructions as if it were a single piece of paper.)

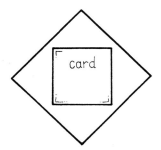
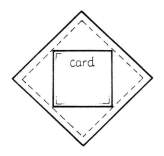

2. Fold the corners in over the card. Take care to fit the envelope closely to the card, but not so tight that it will be a struggle to put it in and take it out.

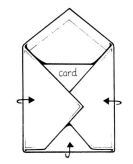

3. Unfold the paper and snip away the triangles that appear along the folds as shown.

4. Refold the paper and glue the side edges in place over the bottom.

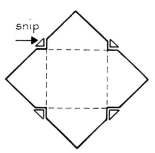

Use a contrasting colour for the lining to give a bold effect.

Make Your Own Gift-wrap

You will need:

★ *large sheets of white cartridge paper*

★ *watercolour paints*

★ *water*

★ *large, soft paintbrushes*

★ *washing line or hanging rod to hang the paper on*

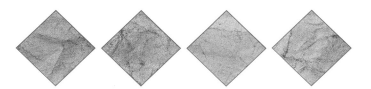

1. Crumple the cartridge paper into a ball. Take care not to tear it, but make sure you crease it all over.

2. Unwrap the paper and smooth it out. Crumple it and smooth it several times till it is well creased all over.

3. Mix one colour of paint with enough water to make colour wash. Brush it on with large, sweeping strokes, and work quickly so the edge of the paint doesn't dry before you paint over it. Notice how the colour is deeper where it sinks into the crease folds.

4. If you wish, apply two or more colours in 'cloud' patterns. Take care to choose colours that mix well together, so you get a pleasing effect where they run into each other. You will need to have all your colours ready at the start, and a paintbrush for each, so you can add a cloud of colour next to the one you have just painted while the edges are still wet.

5. Hang the paper over a line to let it dry.

You can make your paper more glamorous by drawing a simple repeat design with a gold marker pen. Here are some ideas.

Wrapping Gifts

Learn how to wrap a box neatly, following these steps.

You will need:

* ★ *wrapping paper*
* ★ *clear sticky-tape*
* ★ *ruler*
* ★ *pencil*
* ★ *scissors*
* ★ *ribbon or raffia*

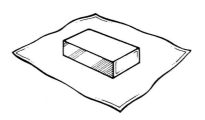

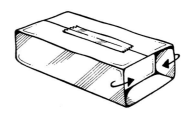

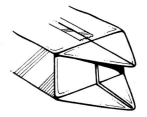

1. Lay the box on the wrapping paper. Cut a rectangle that will wrap around it with 2 cm overlap for the top join and extend each side to create folded ends.

2. Wrap the paper around the box with an overlap like this. Tape as shown. Fold in the side extensions like this.

3. Crease the upper and lower flaps into neat 'V' shapes.

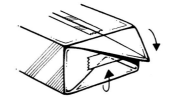

4. Fold the lower 'V' up and tape.

5. Fold the upper 'V' down and tape. Do the same both ends. Add a ribbon to the parcel.

Experiment with different ways of tying ribbon or raffia round a parcel. Curling parcel ribbon is fun to use. To make it curl, run it between your thumb and the edge of a ruler, with the ruler against the back edge. Tie in extra pieces around a knot for an abundance of curls.

Gift Bags

Many gifts are odd-shaped, and don't come in a box. Make smart bags big enough to hold them and disguise their shape!

You will need:

★ *wrapping paper*

★ *clear sticky-tape*

★ *a selection of packs and boxes*

★ *small gifts (sweets, novelty items etc.)*

★ *ruler*

★ *pencil*

★ *scissors*

★ *tissue paper*

★ *hole punch*

★ *ribbon or raffia*

1. Find a box-shaped package as big as the bag you need to make. Cereal packets are a good size.

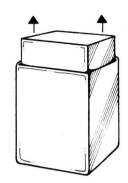

2. Form the bag as if you were wrapping the box itself (see p. 58), but leave one end open. Remove the box.

3. Fold the sides in like this and crease gently.

4. Place the gift inside. You can wrap it in tissue paper, which looks luxurious and holds it more firmly padded inside the bag.

5. Fold the top over and seal it shut.

You can simply tape the flap down; or, as shown here, you can punch two holes and tie it shut.

Christmas Stockings

Many people hang a stocking at the end of the bed at Christmas, knowing that it will be filled with gifts by the morning. Some of the legends of the first Santa Claus, or Saint Nicholas, say that he dropped gifts into a stocking; others say his gifts fell into shoes.

This decorated stocking will surely be filled by the secret gift-bringer who comes to your home!

You will need:

★ *paper*

★ *pencil*

★ *ruler*

★ *pins*

★ *scissors*

★ *needle*

★ *coloured thread*

★ *felt in at least two different colours*

★ *bells, beads and sequins*

★ *oddment of strong yarn*

1. First draw a stocking shape on paper.

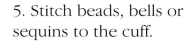

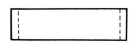

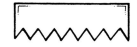

2. Next draw a 'cuff' that is a little more than twice the width of the top of the stocking, so it wraps round the top with about 6 mm extra. Cut it with a plain or zig-zag edge as you wish. Experiment with designs on paper before you start cutting the fabric.

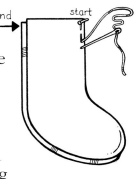

3. Pin the stocking shape to a double layer of felt and cut it out. Pin the cuff shape to a single layer and cut it out.

4. Stitch the two stocking pieces together with a simple in-and-out stitch. Start with a knot, and finish off with a couple of overlapping stitches.

5. Stitch beads, bells or sequins to the cuff.

6. Fold the cuff round the top of the stocking with the edges at the back and stitch in place with a simple in-and-out stitch. Continue stitching to join the two edges of the cuff at the back.

7. Add a hanging loop to the back corner by making a stitch with a length of strong yarn through all thicknesses. Knot the ends.

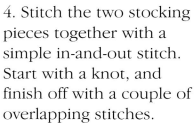

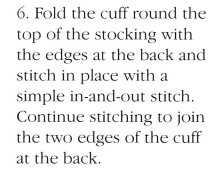

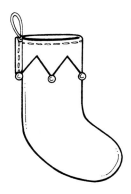

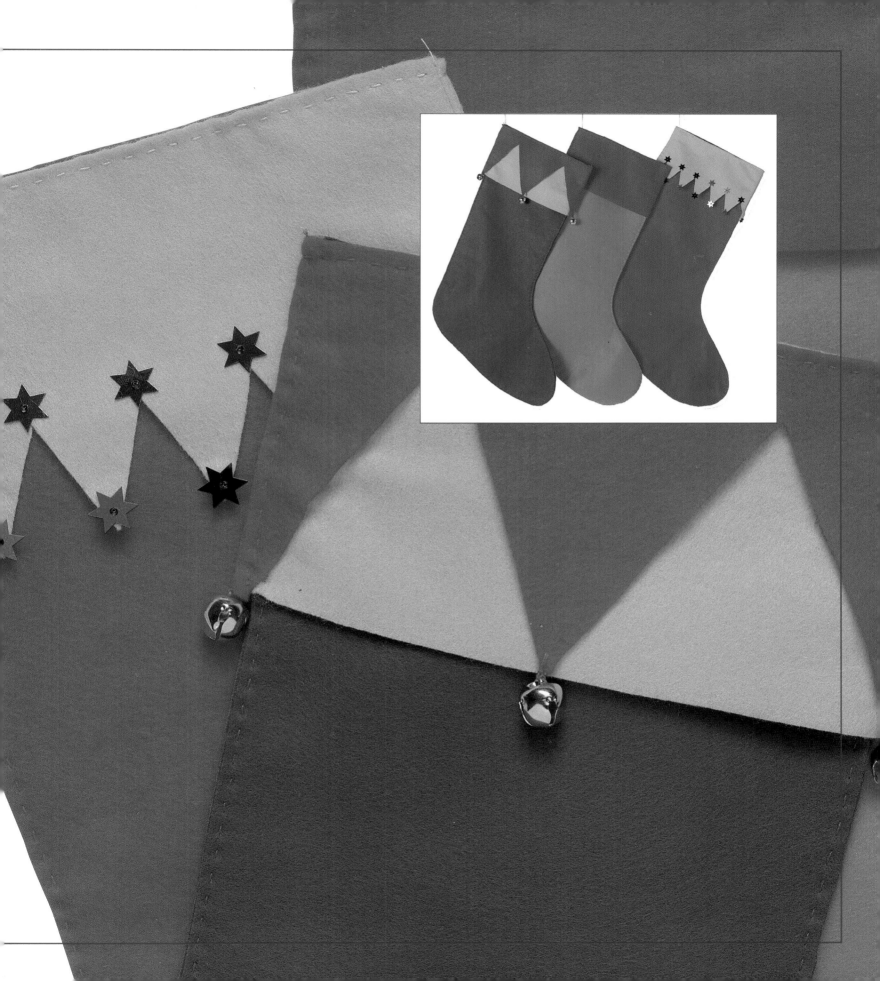

Christmas Gifts

These pretty containers are a gift in themselves. Fill them with sweets or goodies for your friends. Make one for every person who will gather round your Christmas table, and enclose a small surprise gift.

You will need:

★ *thick card*

★ *tracing paper*

★ *pencil*

★ *ruler*

★ *cutting board and craft knife*

★ *paintbrush*

★ *gesso*

★ *sponge*

★ *coloured paints*

★ *coloured yarn or raffia*

★ *sticky-tape*

1. Carefully trace the outline of the shape shown on p. 65.

2. Lay the traced outline on some card, and then go over the lines again, pressing quite heavily with the pencil so the lines show as marks on the card.

3. Cut out the card carefully, using a craft knife against a ruler, to make sure the lines are straight.

4. Lightly score the five lines that mark the base. Fold the sides up along these lines; then flatten the piece again.

5. Paint the card with gesso on one side and leave to dry.

6. Then paint gesso onto the other side and leave that to dry. If the card curls (and it probably will), sandwich the dry card in between two layers of kitchen towel and leave under a heavy book overnight.

7. Sponge or paint a pattern on the card. Leave to dry.

8. Tape one end of a length of yarn to the inside of one of the side strips at the base; then fold the sides up. Begin weaving round and round. If you wish, you can change the colour of yarn by knotting in a new piece, making sure the knot is on the inside.

The containers make great pots for a desk or cupboard.

Copy the shape below to make attractive gift containers.

Decorating the Pots

Instead of making a container from card, you could decorate a flowerpot. Simply paint it with gesso inside and out to start, and then add painted decorations. This one was first sponged all over with gold. Later, the rim was brushed with gold.

Filling the Pots

1. Cut a square of cellophane or tissue paper and push into the container. Experiment to find the size that fits the container and leaves big enough corners to fan out glamorously.

2. Centre the gift on the paper and gather the package carefully in your hands. Gently fit it into the container.

3. Tie the package with yarn or ribbon. Fan out the corners.

You can fit two or three smaller packages into a single container. Wrap them in different coloured paper for an exciting look.

Christmas Goodies

Cinnamon Stars

<u>*You will need:*</u>

★ *1 egg-white*

★ *½ cup granulated sugar*

★ *½ cup ground almonds, plus a little extra*

★ *1 teaspoon cinnamon*

★ *corn starch*

Preheat the oven to 350°F.
Line a baking tray with baking parchment.

1. Whisk the egg-white in a bowl until it is stiff.

2. Whisk in the sugar and keep whisking for about 5 minutes.

3. Spoon about a quarter of the mixture into a separate bowl. Then add the ground almonds and cinnamon to the mixture in the main bowl and stir in. The mixture should be stiff enough to gather into a ball. If it isn't, add more ground almonds—about a tablespoon at a time.

4. Place a piece of baking parchment on a clean work surface and sprinkle corn starch onto it. Place the ball of almond mixture on top. Sprinkle the top of the ball with more corn starch, then roll out the mixture to ¼ inch thickness.

5. Use a star cutter to make stars—or use any shape you like!

6. Carefully lift the biscuit shapes onto the baking tray.

7. Gather up the scraps of almond mixture into a ball and re-roll. Continue making more biscuits until the mixture has been used.

8. Now spoon ¼ teaspoonful of the egg-white and sugar mix into the centre of each biscuit.

9. Bake the biscuits for 8–10 minutes, or until the edges are turning brown. Use oven mitts to lift the tray out of the oven.

10. Leave the biscuits to cool on a wire tray.

Shortbread

You will need:

★ *10 tablespoons butter*

★ *¼ cup granulated sugar*

★ *1 cup plain flour*

★ *3 tablespoons rice flour*

Preheat the oven to 350°F.
Line an 8 inch round tin with baking parchment.

1. Beat the butter and sugar together until creamy.

2. Stir in the flour and rice flour, and keep stirring until the mixture forms a soft ball.

3. Flatten the ball gently in your hands to make a round, then place this in the round tin and press out to the edges.

4. With the blunt edge of a knife, mark into eight wedges. Prick all over with a fork. You can make fancy designs with the pattern of holes if you like!

5. Bake for 35–40 minutes in the oven until golden. Use oven mitts to lift the tin out onto a heatproof surface. Allow to cool for 10 minutes, then hold the parchment to lift the biscuit onto a wire rack. Slide the parchment away and leave the biscuit to cool.

Chocolate Medallions

You will need:

★ *7 ounces plain chocolate*

★ *almonds, pecans, hazelnuts*

★ *glacé cherries and raisins*

★ *paper cases*

1. Break the chocolate into small pieces, and place into a heatproof bowl.

2. Melt the chocolate, either by microwaving on high for 1 minute and then in 10-second bursts, or by placing the bowl in a larger pan of almost boiling water. Stir with a dry spoon so the chocolate is creamy throughout.

3. Arrange the paper cases in muffin tins; then pour a little melted chocolate into each—enough to cover the base ¼ inch deep.

4. Add your selection of nuts and fruit to each medallion.

5. Place in the fridge to cool. Remove the paper cases before serving the medallions.

Christmas Drinks

Festive Lemonade

You will need:

* ★ *lemonade*
* ★ *grapefruit juice*
* ★ *orange juice*
* ★ *glacé cherries*
* ★ *slices of angelica*
* ★ *water*
* ★ *ice-cube tray*

1. Fill the ice-cube tray with water. Add a glacé cherry and one or two pieces of angelica to each cube section. Freeze.

2. When you are ready to serve the drinks, fill each glass one-third full of grapefruit or orange juice. Top up with lemonade.

3. Decorate with festive ice cubes.

Spiced Apple Drink

You will need:

* ★ 4–6 kumquats
* ★ whole cloves
* ★ 1 quart apple juice
* ★ 2 tablespoons honey or brown sugar
* ★ 2 cinnamon sticks

1. Stick the kumquats with cloves in decorative patterns. Put all the ingredients in a large saucepan and warm gently until the mixture is just simmering. Leave to simmer for 5 minutes. Then leave to cool for 5 minutes.

2. Meanwhile, warm some tumblers by filling them with hot water from the tap and leaving them to stand.

3. When you are ready to serve the juice, tip away the water and dry the tumblers with a clean cloth. Spoon one or two kumquats into each glass and pour the warm juice in.

You can easily serve the spiced apple in ceramic mugs which do not need preheating. Leave the spiced drink for only a minute or two before you pour it, as the mugs will cool the drink a little by themselves.

PART 4
Tales and Legends

*Some say that ever 'gainst that season comes
Wherein our Saviour's birth is celebrated,
This bird of dawning singeth all night long;
And then, they say, no spirit dare stir abroad;
The nights are wholesome, then no planets strike,
No fairy takes, nor witch hath power to charm,
So hallowed and so gracious is that time.*

WILLIAM SHAKESPEARE,
HAMLET, PRINCE OF DENMARK, ACT 1, SCENE 1

The Oxen

★

Thomas Hardy (1840–1928)
Illustrated by Elena Gomez

Christmas Eve, and twelve of the clock,
  'Now they are all on their knees,'
An elder said as we sat in a flock
  By the embers in hearthside ease.

We pictured the meek mild creatures where
  They dwelt in their strawy pen,
Nor did it occur to one of us there
  To doubt they were kneeling then.

So fair a fancy few would weave
  In these years! Yet, I feel,
If someone said on Christmas Eve,
  'Come, see the oxen kneel

In the lonely barton by yonder coomb
  Our childhood used to know,'
I should go with him in the gloom,
  Hoping it might be so.

All in Tune

★

Anonymous
Illustrated by Alison Wisenfeld

All in tune to William's flute
Now is Robin's tabor,
Dance tonight and sing high praise
As they did in other days,
Every kindly neighbour.
All in tune, all in tune,
Are the flute and tambourine,
All in tune, all in tune,
Heaven and earth tonight are seen.

God and man are in accord,
More than flute or tabor,
Dance for joy and sing with awe,
For the child upon the straw
Is our God and neighbour.
God and man, God and man,
Are like flute and tambourine,
God and man, God and man,
As true neighbours here are seen.

The Baker's Christmas

★

Christina Goodings
Illustrated by Liz Pichon

Ding, dong! Ding, dong!

It was Christmas night, and the church bells were calling the village folk to come together to hear again the story of the birth of Jesus at the start of their Christmas holiday.

'It's all very well for some people to stop work,' grumbled the baker, 'but people will still want their bread in the morning.'

He pulled on his boots and stamped off through the snow to the kitchen behind his shop.

He heaved open a great sack, and scooped flour into his bowl.

'I suppose I ought to make even more than usual,' he thought moodily. 'I suppose people will be feasting.' So he put in extra flour.

He lifted the cover from a little bowl, and took a spoonful of yeast.

He dipped his hand into a jar, and grasped a handful of salt.

Then he took a jug of water and poured it in to make his dough.

He stirred to the left and he stirred to the right.

He gathered the dough in his hands and squeezed it and pulled it, pushed it and pummelled it, squashed it and flattened it.

At last he had done the kneading. Wearily he wiped his hands.

'Now I must shape the dough into loaves,' he said aloud, and he began to make all kinds of loaves: round loaves and long loaves, plain loaves and plaited loaves.

He filled three great trays with loaves and left them to rise while he built up the fire in the oven.

When he turned round, he could not believe what he saw. It seemed as if the loaves were moving. He rubbed his eyes. 'I must be very tired tonight,' he said. But when he looked again, he was even more baffled.

The loaves had changed shape. Where there had been loaves, there were now tiny children: sitting, and stretching, standing and walking, running and dancing.

As the baker watched in amazement, the children danced right off the tray and across the floor. 'Come back, come back!' ordered the baker.

But the children took no notice. They just went on dancing and spinning right across the floor of his kitchen, through the door and out into the street.

'My bread, my customers,' cried the baker. 'Whatever will become of me if there is no bread in the morning?'

He ran after the dancing children as fast as he could.

They led him down the street, across the square, and up a little hill to the church. The little dough children ran inside, and the baker followed them.

There, in a corner, the village children had gathered around the little scene of the stable in Bethlehem. They were singing a carol, and their eyes were shining with wonder and delight at the sight of Mary and Joseph and the tiny baby. The clay figures were old and shabby, but even so, in the flickering candlelight, they shone with a light so clear and golden it could have been the light of heaven itself.

The dough children joined in the carol. None of the children appeared to notice, but it seemed to the baker that the song had never sounded so clear and tuneful.

As the last chorus echoed into silence, the dough children gathered together and tiptoed out of the church.

Out in the dark night, the baker could hardly see where they went, but he thought it was in the direction of his shop, so he hurried along as fast as he could.

When he got there, everything was calm. There were no dough children to be seen. The loaves on the trays had risen round and plump, just as they always did. The fire in the oven burnt with a cheerful orange glow. The room felt brighter and warmer and more welcoming than the baker could ever remember.

'How lucky I am to have this work to do!' exclaimed the baker. 'Here, in my kitchen, I too will celebrate Christmas.' While the loaves baked in the oven, he brought out flour and sugar, eggs and treacle, spices and raisins, and set to making sweet biscuits.

He chuckled as he rolled out the dough and cut it into fancy shapes. 'A treat for every child,' he said.

The Legend of Saint Nicholas

★

Lois Rock

Illustrated by Helen Cann

The three sisters stood on tiptoe in the streets of Myra. Above the heads of the wedding guests, they could just catch a glimpse of the bride.

'What a lovely dress she has,' sighed the youngest sister.

'What a lovely party she is having,' sighed the middle sister.

'What a lovely home she will have with her husband,' sighed the eldest.

But then one of the wedding ushers came along. 'Make room for the guests; let the guests through,' he ordered. And the sisters had to slip back into the alleyway that led to their home. They had not been invited. They were too poor for the wealthy to count them as friends. They were so poor they knew their father could never afford the dowry that every girl needed if she was to get married.

Back in the tiny dwelling that was their home, they took off their wet shoes and stockings and huddled round the meagre fire of twigs.

'We shall have to beg for our living,' said the youngest sister.

'Or we shall starve,' said the middle sister.'

The eldest sister remained silent. 'What can I do to earn some money for my family?' she worried. 'Will I ever get married?'

Their father returned. 'I walked the streets, taking work wherever I was needed, but this is all the food my wages could buy,' he said sadly. Together they ate a simple meal of bread and soup, trying not to think of the great feast that others were enjoying in the heart of town.

The fire soon burnt low, and night was falling. The sisters had no candle, so they left their shoes and stockings by the hearth and went to bed.

In a great hall in the centre of town, huge torches burnt to illuminate the wedding festivities. Many wealthy people had gathered in their fine clothes to celebrate the wedding. Now they were eating and drinking, singing and dancing.

Among them walked a plainly-dressed man named Nicholas. He was the bishop of the church and had himself performed the wedding ceremony for the young couple. Many of the guests knew him as a friend.

'My dear Nicholas,' called one man, 'thank you so much for visiting my mother when she was ill and I was away on business. Please accept this small gift with our grateful thanks.'

A woman made her way through the crowd to Nicholas. 'My son is so much happier at school now that he can read as well as the others,' she smiled. 'Thank you so much for helping him learn his letters. Please accept this small gift with our grateful thanks.'

The bride's father saw Nicholas from across the hall and strode over. 'It is a privilege to have you at our daughter's wedding,' he cried. 'We are so pleased you were able to perform the ceremony, and ask for God's blessing on my daughter and her new family.' Then, speaking more quietly, he added, 'Please accept this small gift with our grateful thanks.'

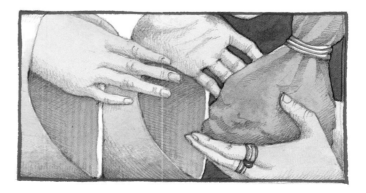

At midnight, while the party was still at its height, Nicholas slipped away into the dark streets. He made his way to the poorer part of town, where few candles flickered at the windows. He came at last to a house that was completely dark, where the three sisters lived with their father.

The wooden shutters were old and broken, and carefully Nicholas pulled one shutter open.

One. Two. Three.

Through the window, Nicholas threw the bags of gold he had been given; then, silently and unseen, he went away.

The following morning, the youngest sister woke first. 'There is a bag of gold in my shoe!' she exclaimed.

The middle sister tumbled from her bed and came to see. 'And look, here is gold in mine,' she cried.

The eldest sister came running and picked up her shoes. 'There is gold in my shoe too,' she whispered, and a tear of happiness slid down her cheeks.

She went out to buy bread and meat and fresh vegetables and wine. That day, as the family gathered around their small feast, their father stood up from the table and said proudly, 'I do not know who has brought us good fortune today; but if that person lives in this town, then they will see what I shall do with the gifts they have given. For I shall arrange a good marriage for each of you, my daughters: first my eldest daughter, second my middle daughter and third my youngest daughter.

'What is more,' he added, 'I shall even ask Bishop Nicholas to perform the wedding ceremony, and pray for God's blessing on each of you.'

The Tale of Three Trees

★

Mary Joslin

Illustrated by Claire St Louis Little

Long ago, on a high hillside, stood three trees. With every passing year, they grew taller and stronger. In the spring, their roots drank in the cool raindrops that trickled through the soil. In the summer, they unfolded their leaves to the sun. In the autumn, strong winds swirled around their branches. In winter, they rested. Snow settled around their roots and on their branches. Under the cold night sky that glittered with a million stars, they dreamed their dreams.

The first tree spoke. 'My dream is of great riches,' it said. 'I want to make them mine and to hold them tight. I do not want to stay out here where the wind strips my branches bare each year; I want to be made into a beautiful chest that will hold the finest treasure.'

The second tree spoke. 'My dream is of great power,' it said. 'I want to have my way wherever I go. I do not want to stay out here rooted to the soil. I want to be made into a mighty sailing ship, and for the world's mightiest kings to put their life into my hands when they sail the great oceans.'

The third tree sighed, and shivered as a chill breeze shook its branches. 'I want to stay here for ever,' it said. 'I want to point to the vast and beautiful heavens, and to the mysteries that lie beyond them.'

Many years went by, and the trees grew ever taller. Then, one winter's day, three woodcutters climbed the hill, and each one had an axe.

'This tree has wood that will last for years,' said the woodcutter who stood under the first tree. He lifted his axe.

'Now I shall hold great treasure,' thought the first tree, and it fell to the ground.

'This tree has wood that is hard and strong,' said the woodcutter who stood under the second tree. He lifted his axe.

'Now I shall carry kings across the sea,' thought the second tree, and it fell to the ground.

'This tree has grown very tall,' said the woodcutter who stood under the third tree. He lifted his axe. 'Now my dream is already over,' wept the third tree, and it fell to the ground.

A carpenter took the wood from the first tree, sawed it into planks, then joined them—not into a chest, but into a trough for cattle-feed. The farmer filled it with hay for his slow, dreamy-eyed oxen. 'What has happened to my dream?' wondered the tree.

One night, the animals were led aside and a man and a woman took shelter in the stable. Soon, gentle hands put fresh, clean straw in the trough, and a new-born baby was laid upon it. Then the first tree knew that it was holding the greatest treasure the world had ever known.

A shipwright took the wood from the second tree. He sawed it and shaped it into a small boat. Fishermen cast their nets from it into a violet blue lake and dragged in their catch of slithering fish. 'What has happened to my dream?' wondered the tree.

One night, storm winds blew and great waves crashed. Then a man stood up in the boat and spoke to the storm: 'Peace. Be still.' At once there was calm, and the second tree knew that it was carrying the mightiest king the world had ever known.

The wood from the third tree was roughly hewn and left in a woodyard.
But the tree had already given up dreaming.

Years passed. The wood was almost forgotten. Then, one day, came a
clamour of voices: 'Any wood will do, but fetch it quickly!'

Rough hands grasped the wood of the third tree, and made it into a
cross. Cruel hands forced a man onto the timbers. Soldiers fastened him to
the wood, with nails through his hands and his feet. Then they hoisted the
cross upright. There, on a low, barren hilltop, the man died.

Three days later, a bright day dawned.

As a gentle morning breeze blew, the tree knew that everything had changed: the man who had died was alive again. Death was no more.

From that day on, whenever people looked at the cross, they lifted their eyes to the vast and beautiful heavens and thought of the mysteries that lie beyond them.

A Christmas Prayer

★

Robert Louis Stevenson (1850–94)
Illustrated by Francesca Pelizzoli

Loving Father, help us remember the birth of Jesus, that we may share in the song of the angels, the gladness of the shepherds and the wisdom of the wise men.

Close the door of hate and open the door of love all over the world.

Let kindness come with every gift and good desires with every greeting.

Deliver us from evil by the blessing which Christ brings and teach us to be merry with clean hearts.

May the Christmas morning make us happy to be your children and the Christmas evening bring us to our beds with grateful thoughts, forgiving and forgiven, for Jesus' sake. Amen.